MAKING THE **STEVE JOBS** MOVIE

MAKING THE
STEVE
JOBS
MOVIE

An Entrepreneurial Case Study

JOE MANCUSO

New York

MAKING THE **STEVE JOBS** MOVIE
An Entrepreneurial Case Study

© 2014 **JOE MANCUSO**. All rights reserved.

All rights reserved. No portion of this book may be reproduced, stored in a retrieval system, or transmitted in any form or by any means—electronic, mechanical, photocopy, recording, scanning, or other,—except for brief quotations in critical reviews or articles, without the prior written permission of the publisher.

Published in New York, New York, by Morgan James Publishing. Morgan James and The Entrepreneurial Publisher are trademarks of Morgan James, LLC. www.MorganJamesPublishing.com

The Morgan James Speakers Group can bring authors to your live event. For more information or to book an event visit The Morgan James Speakers Group at www.TheMorganJamesSpeakersGroup.com.

Front Cover / Interior Photos:
Reproduced with permission from CEO Club International and AllThingsDigital (AllThingsD.com) from footage taken from the documentary film, "Making jOBS: An Entrepreneurial Case Study", produced by CEO Clubs International, Inc.

BitLit
FOR ALL THE BOOKS YOU OWN

FREE eBook edition for your existing eReader with purchase

PRINT NAME ABOVE

For more information, instructions, restrictions, and to register your copy, go to **www.bitlit.ca/readers/register** or use your QR Reader to scan the barcode:

ISBN 978-1-61448-886-6 paperback
ISBN 978-1-61448-887-3 eBook
ISBN 978-1-61448-888-0 audio
ISBN 978-1-61448-889-7 hardcover
Library of Congress Control Number:
2013949954

Cover Design by:
Rachel Lopez
www.r2cdesign.com

Interior Design by:
Bonnie Bushman
bonnie@caboodlegraphics.com

In an effort to support local communities, raise awareness and funds, Morgan James Publishing donates a percentage of all book sales for the life of each book to Habitat for Humanity Peninsula and Greater Williamsburg.

Get involved today, visit
www.MorganJamesBuilds.com.

Habitat for Humanity®
Peninsula and
Greater Williamsburg
Building Partner

Steve Mariotti

In the spirit of entrepreneurship this book is dedicated to my life-long friend, Steve Mariotti.

I meet Steve when he worked for no pay at the CEO Clubs for six years, during which he founded the Network For Teaching Entrepreneurship (www.nfte.com)

Founded in New York City in 1987 by Steve Mariotti, a former entrepreneur turned high school math teacher in the South Bronx, NFTE began as a program to prevent dropouts and improve academic performance among students who were at risk of failing or quitting school.

Steve is an example of the entrepreneurial culture which surrounds the USA colleges and Universities. To date, NFTE has worked with more than 500,000 young people from low-income communities in programs across the United States and around the world.

— **Joseph Mancuso**, Founder, CEO Clubs International

Contents...

ABOUT THE EDITOR...

Joseph R. Mancuso

The founder of the 33 year old not-for-profit Chief Executive Officers Clubs International (CEO Clubs), Joe Mancuso is the entrepreneur's entrepreneur. The CEO Clubs is composed of CEO's running businesses with about $20,000,000 of average annual sales. The club has over 15,000 current active members worldwide.

Mancuso is a popular speaker and participants have paid over $150,000,000 to hear the talks and workshops conducted or arranged by Joseph Mancuso.

Most recently, Joe has traveled to China twenty times in ten years and brought with him on the trips over 800 diverse CEOs. Today the Clubs have chapters in China, India, Greece, and Romania.

Mancuso is undoubtedly best known as an author. His books and tapes have been heard or read by more small business people than those of any other management author, according to Simon & Schuster. He has edited or written twenty-six books, and currently ten books are classified as backlist books, which sell about the same quantity every year. In addition, Joe has authored numerous magazine articles and booklets; in such a diverse magazines as Playboy, Penthouse, Success, Harvard Business Review, The Journal of Marketing and The Journal of Small Business. His materials about business plan preparation have outsold all other authors combined.

Joe holds an Electrical Engineering degree from WPI and an MBA from the Harvard Business School. His Doctorate is from Boston University in Educational Administration. He was the Chairman of the Management Department at Worcester Polytechnic Institute (WPI) in Massachusetts before launching the CEO Clubs in 1977. He lives in Manhattan, with his wife and business partner, Karla, their two children Max and May. His three married daughters have given him six grandchildren.

"It's not the naysayer who changes the world. It's not the critic who points out how the strong man stumbles or where the CEOs could have done it better. The acclaim belongs to the man in the arena: the doer whose face is marred by dust and sweat and blood, the man who spends himself in a worthy cause while striving valiantly, always going uphill."

"These CEOs come up short again and again, but all know the inner warmth of triumph and victory, and they – at worst – fail while daring greatly, for they know their place shall never be with those cold and timid souls who know neither victory nor defeat."

—Joseph Mancuso

PREFACE

"Jobs" (stylized as jOBS) is a 2013 biographical drama film based on the career of late American businessman, Steve Jobs, from 1971 to 2011, produced by Mark Hulme. The CEO Clubs, of which Hulme is a member, is a group of CEOs that has been together for more than three decades and acts as a mutual board of advisers for one another. In mid-October, 2012, Hulme was joined in Santa Fe, New Mexico by fifteen other CEO Clubs members from various unrelated businesses, during which he gave a detailed talk relating his experiences in making the jOBS film.

Mark is a first-time film producer, and had no experience in the film industry prior to the making of jOBS. Like his peers at the meeting, he is a lifelong entrepreneur, and just how his film came about is a fascinating tale of the American entrepreneurial spirit. In addition, the reaction and advice from his buddies makes for an exhilarating documentary.

Where did he find the script? Who is this unknown writer? What part did Craig's List play in the making of Hulme's feature? How did he attract Ashton Kutcher to play Steve Jobs? What role did Mark Hulme's family play in the making of the film?

The USA is unique in the world, in that it's our entrepreneurial culture that is the envy of the world. This documentary is a testament to that.

"Stay hungry. Stay foolish. Your time is limited, so don't waste it living someone else's life. Don't be trapped by dogma—which is living with the results of other people's thinking. Don't let the noise of other's opinions drown out your own inner voice. And most important, have the courage to follow your heart and intuition. They somehow already know what you truly want to become. Everything else is secondary."

—**Steve Jobs**, Stanford University Commencement speech

*Featuring Mark Hulme, Marcos Rodriguez, and members of the Super PAC of CEO Clubs International, Inc.

*Special thanks to AllThingsDigital for footage of Bill Gates and Steve Jobs at the D5 Conference.

jOBS: Be Inspired...

Directed by Joshua Michael Stern
Written by Matt Whiteley

Cast...

Ashton Kutcher	Steve Jobs
Dermot Mulroney	Mike Markkula
James Woods	Jack Dudman
Ronnie Gene Blevins	Dealer
Ron Eldard	Rod Holt
Matthew Modine	John Sculley
Lukas Haas	Daniel Kottke
J.K. Simmons	Arthur Rock
Amanda Crew	Julie
Josh Gad	Steve Wozniak
Ahna O'Reilly	Chris-Ann Brennan
Lesley Ann Warren	Clara Jobs
Elden Henson	Andy Hertzfeld
David Denman	Al Alcorn
Kevin Dunn	Gil Amelio

Clint Jung	Gareth Chang
Victor Rasuk	Bill Fernandez
Ava Acres	Young Lisa Jobs
Hollie Winnard	Rod Holt's Wife
John Getz	Paul Jobs
Brad William Henke	Paul Terrell
Brett Gelman	Jeff Raskin
Nelson Franklin	Bill Atkinson
Clayton Rohner	Financial Expert
Scott Krinsky	Homebrew Attendee
Eddie Hassell	Chris Espinosa
Giles Matthey	Jonathan Ive
Lenny Jacobson	Burrell Smith
Mark Kassen	Jud
Annika Bertea	Lisa Jobs
Evan Helmuth	Francis
Laura Niemi	Jobs' Secretary
Jim Turner	Jobs' Attorney
Kent Shocknek	1980 News Caster
Hazel Dolphy	Apple Employee
Debra Garrett	Apple Executive
Lanre Idewu	Apple Executive
Alan D. Purwin	Helicopter Pilot
Dan Shaked	Apple Engineer #2
Joe Filippone	Atari Employee
Aaron Webster	Hewlett-Packard Employee
Rachel Rosenstein	Apple Receptionist
Aaron Kuban	Ethan
DeRick Walker	Classmate
Nick Pasqual	Mac Design Team Member
Cody Chappel	Student at Lounge

Abigail McConnell	Joanna Hoffman
Ness Bautista	Dealer #2
Rodney J. Richards	Professor
Paul Borst	Apple Employee
Zachary Tupaz	Kurt Louis
Matthew Scott Hill	Design Engineer (uncredited)
Maksim Kovalev	Press Crew Member (uncred.)
Samm Levine	Apple Designer (uncred.)
Adam C Smith	Mac Designer (uncred.)

Produced By...

Ronald Bulard	Executive Producer
Gil Cates Jr.	Co-Producer
Mark Hulme	Executive Producer
Mark Hulme	Producer
Bill Johnson	Executive Producer
Mark Benton Johnson	Line Producer
Jacob Pechenik	Executive Producer
Marcos Rodriguez	Executive Producer
Jim Seibel	Executive Producer
David C. Traub	Executive Producer
Alton Walpole	Line Producer

Original Music by John Debney
Cinematography by Russell Carpenter
Film Editing by Robert Komatsu
Casting by Mary Vernieu
Production Design by Freddy Waff

—Faster than a foreclosure,
—More powerful than an interoffice memo,
—Able to buy tall buildings with a single check,
  and who, disguised as a mild-mannered···

Either I'm an entrepreneur
or I'm unemployed.

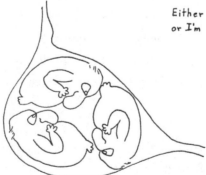

First one out is an entrepreneur!

INTRODUCTION

America's Ecological Entrepreneurial Culture

A hundred years ago Henry Ford, Thomas Edison, John Burroughs, Harvey Firestone used to meet at the Wayside Inn in Sudbury, Massachusetts. Today, groups like our CEO Clubs continue to bring CEOs together "to make money and have fun while we are learning". The USA is unique in the world, and it's our entrepreneurial culture that is the envy of the world.

I have taken over 1000 CEOs to other countries, mostly China, to do business. Do you think any of these countries want to copy our legal system? Or our political system? Or our movie system? The answer is no. But they do envy our educational system; many foreign students opt to get their education in the USA. But it is not simply the colleges and universities which hold appeal. It is what surrounds our educational system.

Yet both Steve Jobs and the hero of this documentary (Mark Hulme) never finished college. So, why do foreigners choose to educate their children here?

It's our entrepreneurial system that allows the USA to be the only country that could create and reward a Steve Jobs, or Bill Gates, or Larry Ellison, or Dave Packard, or a couple of my all-time favorites Ted Turner or Fred Smith and the list goes on and on.

Enjoy this book and see how this unique entrepreneurial American ecosystem works. There are no actors. This is a live unedited dialogue with no retakes. It's our educational system at work.

CEOs work and play hard and you will see a dozen of them sharing ideas among peers.

I promise you will gain insight into: Steve Jobs, Apple, and the American Entrepreneurial system. It is truly unique in the world. It is America's most exportable product. This documentary will show you this system live and in person. And it is fun. It creates "Steve Jobs" moments.

Have you ever driven past an empty lot and suggested to a friend it would be a great place for a car wash? Have you ever passed an empty retail location and said, "What a great place to build a restaurant"? Then one day when someone builds one, and you say, "I should have..."

Did you ever say, "I could make that movie?"

PROLOGUE...

Making jOBS: An Entrepreneurial Case Study opening dialogue (taken from the movie jOBS)...

Jobs

Revolution. No more decks, no more mainframes... it changes everything! For your own, for you. It what's you get, it's what you wanted. Instinct. Your brain wanted something that didn't exist, and willed it into existence. What do you call the system?

Woz

The operating system? Yeah, just a real time display operation.

Jobs

You can see what you're working on while you're working on it. But this is freedom. This is freedom to create. To do and to build as artists, as individuals.

Woz

Hey look, you're overreacting. Even if you were developing this for freaks like us, and I doubt you are. Nobody wants to buy a computer. Nobody.

Jobs

How does somebody know what they want if they've never seen it?

FOLLOWING
DIALOGUE SPEAKERS

David W. Bower, Sr.
CEO
Data Computer Corp of America

Gayle A. Glosser
President
Regal Research & Mfg. Co.

Mark C. Hulme
CEO
DS News, Producer of iJOBS

Roy Jones
CEO
Low Cross Farm

Jeffrey Layne
President
Arc-Com Fabrics, Inc.

Joseph R. Mancuso
CEO
CEO Clubs, Inc.

Mike Powell
CEO
Regal Research & Mfg. Co.

David W. Pruitt
CEO
Cap Rock Electricity

Ron Reuven
CEO
Reuven Enterprises

Marcos A. Rodriguez
Chairman
Rodriguez Capital Holdings

Michael Sheaffer
President
Hi-Line, Inc.

John W. Spargo
Chairman
J. Spargo & Associates, Inc.

Mancuso

When did you get the idea to create a Steve Jobs movie?

This is October, 2012.

Hulme

Doesn't everyone want to create a Steve Jobs movie?

[Chuckle]

I was looking around to be an investor in a film but I had heard horror stories about the creative accounting in that business.

So I wanted to find something in film where I could control the checkbook.

I heard that this creative accounting would result in you not getting your money back, so I looked for something that if I lost my money I would at least get a "learning experience"

There was a project I was looking at but I had no interest in the story line.

I would be joining a smart group of savvy film people and my contribution was to be $500,000.

I even sent the script to my attorney.

Then as I am walking down the hall in August, 2011 some art directors and IT people were abuzz by a water cooler.

The excitement of this group leads me to believe it was caused by another 9/11 or a terrorist act.

No, I found out they were discussing the news that Steve Jobs had retired.

Imagine that?

Someone who does not work in Texas and has no association with my magazine publishing businesses could interrupt my companies work output.

I was shocked.

Who is this guy?

He changed the world in so many industries, computers, music, phones, and on and on.

In fact, every time Apple sneezed it made news.

They were and still are so smart that no one does it better.

Now, that is when I want to be a movie investor... that is the story I want to tell.

It all came to me as I was still at the water cooler.

I want to tell the story about Steve Jobs.

Mancuso

When was that?

About fall of 2011?

Hulme

No that was the summer of 2011.

So I dinged the writer in September and asked if he was up to doing a movie script about Steve Jobs.

He worked for me writing advertising copy but I knew he had training in script writing.

We had lunch and he said, "I am up to it, let's go!"

I knew script writing was a rare talent.

I had seen so many million dollar movies with lousy dialogue.

I remain perplexed, how can those lines remain in this $30,000,000 film?

Don't you agree?

So many movies are so badly written yet they can be big successes.

I knew he needed help as this was going to be a big task.

Like me, this writer, Matthew Whitely, idolized the accomplishments of Apple as we used Apple products in all my businesses, book and magazine publishing, and conferencing, bringing our readers to major events.

On some of our major foreclosure conferences, we had George and Laura Bush as headliners.

At another we had Bill Clinton.

All our promotions were done on Apple products.

It was, and still is, an amazing company, and the hero of Apple was Steve Jobs.

In fact, Joe, I heard the CEO Clubs had voted him the most admired CEO in the world.

Is that true?

Mancuso

Yes, and he surpassed both Warren Buffett and Jack Welsh, getting more votes than the two of them combined.

So what day are we at during this stage?

Hulme

It was 2011.

Mancuso

Was it fall of 2011?

Hulme

No, it was summer.

I was willing to risk about a half million in the movie business and I decided I could put that at risk if the story was about Jobs.

So I hired three entry level researchers to help the writer.

We cleared out an office space and called it "The Jobs Research Center".

We rented some temporary furniture.

We had flow charts, pert charts, pictures, and diagrams all over the walls.

It looked like a war room.

But I should tell this group: after all, it is about transparency in this Super PAC, Matt Whitely is my son.

He is the writer who wrote the Jobs movie script.

He is just 24 years old.

It is the only little bit of nepotism I have but I didn't want everyone to know he is my son.

You know how people view that!

Mancuso

Yeah, there is a group somewhat competitive to CEO Clubs based in Chicago.

Its called Sons of Bosses or SOBs.

I hear it is a pretty fun group.

Hulme

By the way, I want everyone to keep this quiet.

Please respect this little bit of inside information.

I bet Ashton Kutcher to this day does not know that Matt Whitely is my son.

No one knows.

Oh, Marcos knows and the director knows, but really no one else.

So, please don't violate that piece of confidentiality.

His full name is Matt Whitely Hulme.

His grandfather made me promise to return his real name eventually, as he is the grandfather.

I agreed.

Mancuso

So at this stage how much money are we in for now?

A half million?

Hulme

No, not that much.

But I figured we had better buy some original Apple computers because we would need them for the movie.

So, we bought them, the writing started coming out, and we watched as everything moved forward.

I figured if the script was bad or we hit a road block we would stop.

We would keep going until we could not go anymore.

The encouraging news is that this is not a western or an old period movie that needs costumes.

Hell, it's about the last forty years, and all we need are some leisure suits.

I still have some of them in my closet.

I knew we could not tell the entire life of Jobs, which would be an HBO miniseries; so we decided to do the movie about a young Steve Jobs and end it when he walked onto the stage to introduce the iPOD.

It is not about when he could do no wrong.

It is about his early life which is so much more colorful and interesting.

It is about how he launched the first computer company and his partner, Wozniak says, "No one wants to buy a computer. No one."

And Jobs replies, "How does someone know what they want if they have never seen it?"

Mancuso

Ok, we have the early idea about your film.

So we are in early fall of 2011 and your team is researching and producing pages of script.

So, you are spending money pretty fast.

What if someone big was also doing that and could beat you to the punch?

Hulme

That never happened so we just kept going.

Mancuso

Ok, then I want to swing over to your lifelong friend, Marcos Rodriguez.

Didn't you once work for him in Dallas?

Was that during the time of you being more of a printer and advertising agency?

Hulme

Yes, Marcos owned the largest Christian Music Radio Station in the country, in Dallas, WKLTY and I became the general manager.

That is when we grew close as friends.

In fact, it was about that time, in the mid-1980s that we both became active in the Dallas Chapter of the CEO Clubs.

We have remained pretty good friends ever since.

In fact, my memory of a CEO Club Super PAC in Dallas still makes me smile.

The evening dinner was being hosted by Sonia and Marcos at their home close to the Four Seasons in Dallas.

I recall it was an out door dinner on one of their terraces.

Actually, the food was great the weather was perfect, but the highlight of the evening was when my rented folding chair collapsed and I landed with a big thud.

No one was hurt, except Sonia felt terrible, but I still recall the other CEOs saying, "Do it again!"

[Laughter]

Mancuso

Ok, let us swing the cameras over to Marcus and have him pick up the story in the fall of 2011.

I think Marcos, living with his family in a log cabin on a hill in Aspen, came to Dallas over Thanksgiving to celebrate the holidays with Sonia's family.

Is that right?

Rodriguez

Yeah, that is right.

I was staying at the Four Seasons and I called Mark and said, "Can you come over for breakfast?"

So, we talked a little, and that's when I found out about the Jobs movie, and I became excited.

I figured, I know about what makes him [Jobs] tick and I really liked the concept of the big idea.

Later, I realized everybody in the world thinks they know Steve Jobs and that is the strength of the idea.

I realize now that a billion people think they hear the music in his head.

I even remember sending a few emails after we meet about my insights into the complicated mind of Steve Jobs.

And Mark invited me to be involved in the film and appointed me CFO.

Hulme

Yeah, I figured I don't know anything about making a movie, so why don't I partner up with another person who doesn't know anything about making a movie.

Pretty smart, Huh?

Mancuso

Yeah, I heard the two of you purchased a book called, "How To Make A Movie".

Hulme

Yeah, we had several books but I will tell you the best source is Wikipedia... in thirty minutes you can find out 90% of what you need to know to make a movie.

Rodriguez

I was pretty animated about Jobs, I was fired up about working with Mark, and it was an exciting breakfast.

Mancuso

Ok, do you want me to leave it there?

Rodriguez

It goes downhill from there, smiling.
[Group laughs]

Mancuso

You mean we just cannot say, "And the rest was history?"

Hulme

I call this a "Steve Jobs" moment, and I had one as Marcos and I finished breakfast.

Jobs had an uncanny ability to enter an area of business where he had zero background and take charge of the issues.

How can one person change so many businesses where he had no real prior skill?

It is sort of me and Marcos entering the film business.

Jobs had an incredible sense of self confidence, really fearlessness, and was never concerned about failure.

May I say, in all humility, making a good film is really a gargantuan task, and it's interesting we are holding this session before the film has been released.

If it's a bad film, so what, get back in there and duke it out and pick yourself up and so what, it's not the end of the world.

But what I am seeing and hearing is it's a great film and all the feed back to me has been positive.

But let's hear what the members who have patiently heard this story have for advice.

Mancuso

Ok, let us open it to member questions.

Mark, about how much money have you invested at this stage?

It sounds like a half million dollars?

Hulme

No, it's much less probably less than $100,000... after all, the researchers are entry level and I haven't had to buy costumes, horses, or big scenery.

It wasn't something I couldn't walk away from and figure I had put my toe in the water.

At this stage I was reading dialogue about this man who we all have enormous respect for, you may not like him, but certainly everyone has respect for his achievements.

You may not like him and, in fact, it is hard to like him.

That's when I decided I had to see this movie.

So, I had to up the ante and figure out how to produce this movie and not bankrupt myself?

That would be tragic.

Here I am running a huge conference and publishing business, publishing books about foreclosures, and then it comes out that I go bankrupt making a movie!?

How embarrassing would that be?

So, I figured I could shoot it in Dallas non-union, and risk two million dollars.

Of course, the actors would have to be union.

Remember this is a period movie, 70-80s and I still have a lot of those leisure suits in my closet.

So I figured that movie could be shot for two million dollars.

Mancuso

That's what we call smoking your own dope.

[Group laughs]

Hulme

Yeah, I can talk myself into anything but that is how I got here in the first place.

I can justify about anything... really, I can.

I hear distribution is difficult; but don't I have a captive audience with all these Mac heads and Apple followers?

I don't want to insult anyone but I am not a Mac head, I am an enthusiast.

I had a few working for me.

These are the folks that follow every word from Apple like a religion.

They keep track of the stock price and the market capitalization.

Does anyone know the market cap for Pepsi or Ford Motors?

No! - And most Mac heads do not even own a share of Apple stock.

Crazy, isn't it?

Mancuso

How do you plan to sell the movie?

How can I buy the movie?

Hulme

Today we are all connected electronically now.

The world has changed and the whole world is connected.

In fact, Joe, if you were to sing a song and record it you could sell it all around the world.

You could do it for $35.00... put it on iTUNES... millions of folks are doing it everyday.

The game has changed radically.

You can be a publisher or a producer, no issue.

I could mail out DVDs, but because we are a no-name we could not get into Wal-Mart; but we would be the only folks with a Steve Jobs story.

If it is any kind of respectable movie you can get some level of distribution.

The tough part of movie making is getting distribution into about 2,000 screens.

So I figured I could get most of my money back, say up to $2,000,000 even with marginal distribution.

The problem is I was testing the waters with probably the best movie script I could ever get my hands on.

I don't see anyway I could do better than the Jobs script.

The writing continues, we keep going, and then Steve Jobs dies.

It was October of 2011 when he dies.

It was a somber time.

We have four people working day and night and the whole company knows about our work.

We knew his retirement meant his health was frail.

But we never thought it was that frail.

Actually at that time I was thinking how intimidating it would be if he was alive and came out with negative comments about our film.

Especially, someone like Steve Jobs; he does not pull any punches.

***

Mancuso

OK, lets open up for questions for those nice folks sitting quietly listening to Mark's intriguing story.

***

Sheaffer

Tell me about your Mom and Dad; how they felt about what you were doing?

***

Hulme

My Mom handled the finances and my Dad was a PR guy.

He was President of the Rotary Club.

My Mom was a zero risk-taker; she would always tell me to go back to school and get my teaching certificate, and I could always fall back on teaching.

Can you imagine her telling me that all her life?

She was a zero risk-taker.

She would not relent... never...

[Laughter]

But they are good folks and I would not be here without their support.

***

Spargo

Loved to have heard these comments a few years before I became involved in the movie business.

I got involved for different reasons, but the way you are approaching it, is what I should have done.

I didn't keep my eye on all the contracts, cash flow, and things like that.

_____

Hulme

How did it work out for you?

_____

Spargo

I got to go to quite a few fun parties.

I got quite a few fun trips to Los Angeles.

I had some memorable weekends in Manhattan with the female star of the movie.

Actually, it was her first movie and we hoped it would help launch a movie career for her.

I wasn't doing it for the right reason.

_____

Hulme

How much did you invest?

_____

Spargo

About $400,000 if you don't count all the trips and parties and hotel rooms.

If you count everything, it's closer to $500,000.

_____

Hulme

Did you make any money on the movie?

_____

Spargo

It was called The Numbers Game and had a few well known actors and a well known director.

There were thirty actors in the movie.

Director:
James Van Alden
Writer:
James Van Alden
Stars:
Madison Walls, Steven Bauer, Ken Howard

Hulme

How much did you make?

Spargo

Nothing.

Hulme

Nothing?
That was a short answer.
[Smiles]

Spargo

It was not what I had hoped; but Madison and I remain friends even today.

I also did some smaller investing in other films.

Never really did well in any of them either.

But I was the producer, like you, for The Numbers Game.

We got into Blockbusters but it never reached it's potential.

I certainly will see your movie no matter how it gets distributed.

I will buy one.

Hulme

Now I need another few million people to say that as well.

Layne

I remember attending a meeting recently where the subject was investing in restaurants.

It strikes me that there is a tremendous parallel with movie and restaurant investing.

How old is your son?

Hulme

He is 24.

Layne

And he wrote the script? - That's an amazing story.

Hulme

Hardly anyone knows that.

We used his middle name, Matt Whitely, as I did not want to be the Dad who is trying to launch his son's career.

We leveled with the director Joshua Michael Stern.

And some insiders like Marcos but I am sure Ashton Kutcher has no idea that Matt Whitely is actually Matt Whitely Hulme.

The agencies like William Morris and CAA also are clueless.

In fact the agencies said, "Wow, where did you find this writer?"

You know the agencies just want to pitch their talent; after all, they are really nothing but sales people.

They are just hawking their wares.

I like salespeople but they say in Hollywood it all starts with the script.

Sure enough it does.

The script opened up the doors.

So, I may be one of the first fathers ever to make money from his offspring - wouldn't that be something?

Any of you here make money off your kids?

_____

Layne

You realize that if you ever do this again, you won't be able to afford him?

_____

Hulme

I offered him a second film.

He had the nerve to say, "let me think about it".

I said, "Matt, are you kidding me?"

So I kinda strong armed him.

I offered him like a standard rate; you know he just makes a writer's pay now, but I offered him $300,000.

_____

Layne

Does he have a contract.

_____

Hulme

No, everyone is a work-for-hire, just commission everyone for a specific work rather than drawing contracts, that's the way to go.

If you commission it, you can more easily make the changes you need to make.

It's the better way to go.

It's the low-budget way.

We will talk about it later; the question is, should I ever do another movie?

Anyway, I offered Matt $300,000 for the next script.

I will only do one or two more films with him as folks were asking me could I contact the writer.

Whitely is my Mom's maiden name.

He is pleased that he has not been judged as just his dad's son... he likes the name Matt Whitely.

I told him that his granddad, my father, made me promise to return his name to Hulme when the Jobs movie finishes.

He may fight me on that as he is enjoying being in his own world.

One time walking off the set with him, because this movie has become so well known and so viral... I said, "If we bomb, I am going to have a hard time showing my face in town".

My son said, "Yeah, but Matt Whitely does not have that problem. I can just vanish into the night".

I should have taken a pen name for the producer, but I never thought of it.

Pruitt

Mark, who selected the actor to play Jobs?

Hulme

Well when we started writing, and I wanted to keep expenses to a controllable level, I figured we should use a talented no-name actor to play Steve.

It is such a huge role in this biopic.

In fact, 45% of the dialogue is Steve Jobs.

So, we'd really better have a no-name play that role or we will get out of control pretty quickly.

Rodriguez

It is ok if he is a no name as long as he looks like George Clooney.
[Laugther]

Hulme

Yeah, right, can't forget that... we may have had more of an artistic, pure film if we hadn't gone so commercial.

And now in October 2012 it's so viral, we no longer control publicity.

We never had Ashton Kutcher in mind.

When we found our director, Joshua Michael Stern and we were working the script - which means cutting back and cutting back and cutting back - we sent it to CAA and William Morris and United talent agency... In fact, I meet with all three of the big dogs in one day.

They all had their books and were all ready to go.

Pruitt

Did you pick the actor for Jobs or did those smart guys from Hollywood pick him?

Hulme

Well these agents are sales people so they just recommended their talent.

Remember they are basically managing the careers of their talent.

They all had to agree to read the script first.

Like I said, it's all about the script and we got such strong revues at these sessions that the doors just flew open.

We told them we were shooting during this range of time, so they only submitted to those which were open during that time slot.

And according to Ashton Kutcher's business manager, Ashton and our director Joshua Michael Stern are both represented by the big dog CAA.

So today, CAA represents the film.

Ashton had heard about the film and he already saw himself in this role.

He is a dead-ringer for the young Steve Jobs.

Plus he is a huge Apple and Steve Jobs fan.

He has been an Apple shareholder for ten years and he is invested in over 50 high tech silicon-valley firms.

He is known for his brilliance, and last year alone he earned $50,000,000.

Of course, his brilliance doesn't always show as he is often cast in screwball comedies and romantic movies.

So, for him, this was the role of a lifetime.

He wanted it so bad.

He was ready.

Kutcher read the script on Monday, and the director meet with him on Wednesday, and I was in CAA office on Friday, and his agent says Ashton is waiting by the phone.

So we said, "Let's roll!"

_____

Glosser

I was wondering how a no-name from Dallas could attract a director like Joshua Michael Stern?

He is a very powerful director, so, I wonder how you could ever just get in contact with him?

_____

Hulme

That is a great question.

Who are we in Dallas?

So we just kept moving to the next step to see what develops.

Our budget was still $2-3 million, but that is it, and we could just shoot it here in Dallas.

We called the agent for Gus Van Zandt and other directors we had heard about.

The problem is in Hollywood there are so many nuts coming out of the woodwork... who are we but just another faint voice in the wilderness.

We didn't have a website... if we did what would it say: another Hollywood nut with no credits to our name.

Like every other wannabe producer, the website would say we are nice people but we have never done anything... yet.

Everyone I spoke to said, send me a script.

But I decided like Pruitt told me at coffee, I am not sending a script, I want to meet with someone and have face to face conversations.

After all, these agents are just salespeople.

Now, I love those salespeople who generate revenue, but I am not going to send them a script.

If they were literary agents it might be different but these agents are just hawking their talent.

So, I never sent the script out.

Instead I did what any entrepreneur would do, I ran an ad on Craigslist.

[Crowd Laughter]

I just ran it in LA, and the director said please don't tell anyone about this... please.

_____

Mancuso

What section of Craigslist has movie directors?

_____

Hulme

Oh, sure, there is a place for it.

We didn't mention Steve Jobs.

We said, "Looking for undiscovered brilliant movie director for an epic biopic. New studio out of Dallas".

I do not know how many mail bags of mail I received.

Rodriguez

You know that at any single period, 99% of Hollywood is unemployed.

What you should have said was enclose $5 with your response

Now, that is a better business model than you will get by financing a movie.

And craigslist is free.

Really, it is a no-brainer.

[Laughter]

Layne

You know I always hear that in Hollywood there is back room accounting and mysterious under the table money... are you worried about those issues?

Hulme

Sure I have heard the same thing and you see all the litigation going on all the time.

You hear about producers who sold their film and never received any money back.

Actually, we are not at that place yet, but there are collection agencies in place now who take say ½ of a point and that cleans up some of the issues.

The best is your foreign sales.

That is so crucial, as how much you receive from say Nigeria or Germany or China is tough to measure; but your foreign distributor is key.

Actually, this is not an academic issue.

Our foreign sales agency, which did a terrific job, went into chapter eleven due to issues not involving our deal.

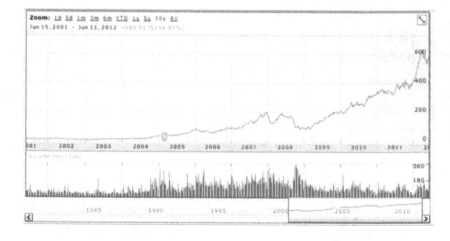

Even in bankruptcy these collection agents were able to keep our money and it really had no effect on our deal.

That tells you how important these collection agencies are in practice.

All those contracts are on deposit with the collection agencies.

They get their percentage but they protect that money.

In fact, those contracts are all solid and they are bankable.

Mancuso

Clear that up.

How could you get the money if the selling agency goes into chapter eleven?

What makes you a preferred creditor?

Hulme

No, only the selling agency goes into chapter eleven.

The contracts themselves go to the foreign collection companies which are separate from the sales agent.

Where you really get in trouble is when you just sell your film and you lose control of the contracts and the money.

What happens that causes the issues is the studio tries to charge all their overhead to your film and pretty soon you make nothing.

I have been told by CAA that the issue is not creative accounting, it's creative contract writing.

It's all in the contracts and none of the long contracts drawn up in Hollywood is good for you, just for them.

It's the ambiguities in the contract that allows them to charge excessive overhead to your film.

I think Marcos can talk to this part, as the industry is bloody and slippery and you lose control very quickly.

Even those people in the industry whose job is to monitor the money and keep the film in budget fail miserably.

Everyone bows down to the director.

The director has one objective in mind and its not running a solid profitable business.

It is a catch-22.

Should I risk more money to make more money or quit now and take a more modest profit?

It seems to be a new issue everyday.

Its' not a pleasant process at all.

So that is the real dilemma, and most producers soon lose control to the director.

Reuven

So the director from Craigslist and your son the writer are all within budget.

Then how did you get Ashton Kutcher all under your two million dollar budget?

Hulme

No, that did not work...

[Laughter]

But it sure doesn't sound like a strong team, does it?

Reuven

Then you have this business under the umbrella of all your other businesses and you rent some cheap furniture.

Hulme

No, that did not work with Kutcher and it didn't work with the director either.

The director is union and he has his agent and his attorney... and, by the way, do not say he was hired because of craigslist.

This is an A-plus director and he said he never saw the craigslist ad but someone told someone who told someone and we are lucky to have him.

And do not say to anyone that he came because of craigslist... ok?

_____

Mancuso

Ok, when will it be in a movie theater or when can I pay $10 to see it on DVD?

_____

Hulme

Originally, we were going at a good speed and the industry is full of producers and wannabe producers who will kick the can down the street forever; but thank goodness for my ADD (attention deficit disorder).

I am not like that... Joe, I remember you sold a T-shirt for entrepreneurs... what did it say?

Do you still sell them?

_____

Mancuso

You have a good memory, but we no longer sell them.

Actually we sold two [kinds].

Entrepreneur T-Shirt:
<Ready-Fire-Aim>

CEO T-shirt:
On the front...
<I am their leader>
On the back...
<Where have they gone?>

Hulme

Well, we were just going full speed ahead and multi-tasking, and I figured we would be in theaters before year end, and we would be eligible for an academy award.

Ashton and CAA were on board with that timetable but because of some hiccups on the post production side, its clear the film won't be ready until December 2012.

Actually, films are made or lost in post production, it always takes longer, and cost more than budgeted.

All the foreign release is tied into the USA release, so it will open worldwide on the same day.

My thought was to release it on Steve Jobs birthday which is February 24th.

We should discuss that at the mastermind.

I would like to get your opinion.

So, I think we will be in theaters no later than the first week in March.

Then it's about 90 days after theater release that it comes out in DVD.

Mancuso

Ok, let's take a break, but first, let's ask John Spargo to hold up his half million movie, and at lunch we can all touch his DVD... Ok John?

Maybe we will pass along good charm.

Spargo

We had some fairly well know actors... Ken Howard has been in a number of movies, and Steve Bauer from Scarface.

Hulme

Yeah, it is always good to have some actors.

I don't know much but I do know actors are essential.

[Laughter]

Spargo

Actually, my movie was put together as a promotional piece for Madison who was the female star of the movie.

The budget went from under $100,000 to over $400,000 just as you said.

Mancuso

Did you recover much.

Spargo

No.

Hulme

That's a quick simple answer.

[Smiling]

Mancuso

John, is this the way you should have done the numbers game? Slow and steady keeping costs under control?

Spargo

Absolutely, I was not focused as Mark is focused.

I should have been more diligent.

I did sit in during a week of the shooting, but I was not able to control costs.

The director had an insatiable appetite to spend money.

He wanted to hire more equipment, but I vetoed that one; but it seems every idea he ever had he wanted to execute in this movie.

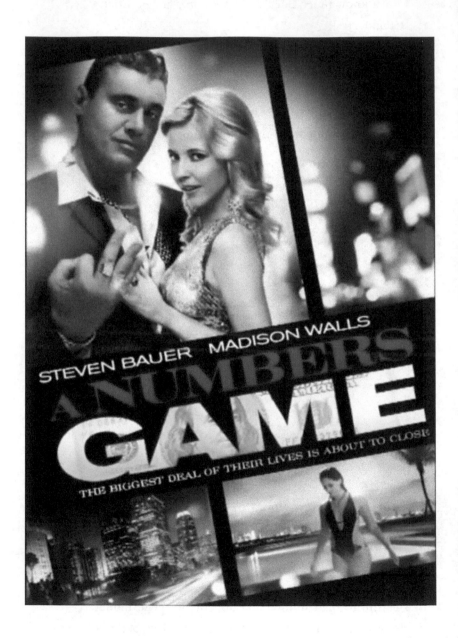

The one place I failed myself was I didn't do a cameo.

Now, I wish I had done that.

Hulme

We actually filmed all the early parts of the movie in the actual garage where Apple was created.

We had to renovate it and restore it to its earlier look but we rented the garage to keep our movie authentic.

Ironically, that garage is just seven minutes from Apples headquarters.

We converted the garage door to the old two folding doors.

What felt so good was it imbedded the story and it actually became a spiritual experience?

We were able to memorialize it.

Eventually the house and the garage will be razed.

Rodriguez

I would like to comment on the theme.

To me its genius is an outlier.

We often look back at exceptional people like Jobs and remember that extremely genius persons are going to have a dark side.

He is the type of person who doesn't fit in, he is a nonconformist.

I look at one of my sons who I think has that same type of personality and I find I have to remind some of his teachers about the two sides of the same coin.

Schools usually don't recognize this type of person, and I find myself over and over reminding his teachers about this type of person.

In a school environment there is pressure to conform, just like in society.

There's a lot of people who like Jobs hear their own music in their heads.

These are often the exceptional people.

He was not only a genius and nonconformist, but he fought extremely hard to get the world to change, to be more like the music he heard in his head.

Mancuso

Well said.

Hulme

Yes — Well said.

Mancuso

What about Wozniak?
Steve Wozniak.

Hulme

Yes, we made him an offer but we lost him to Sony.

Interesting... because there is a big international film festival in the Riviera.

It is the grand daddy of all movie events, Canne film festival.

Actually, that is where we sold most of our foreign rights.

Our sales agency was with us and the Sony executives who really never took us seriously saw that we were selling like hot cakes.

It was during that week that Sony did two separate press releases about their Steve Jobs movie.

Even though the giant Sony corporation has hundreds of things to sell, suddenly they grew concerned about us.

Talking about reacting and running scared, even CAA agreed that they hated to see our success because we could possibly rain on their parade.

They dinged Aron Sorkin, the writer who did The Social Network, but he only...

Mancuso

Is that the fellow who is with the NY Times and on CNBC in the morning?

Hulme

No, he did West Wing and he is under contact to Sony for the Jobs movie.

He is a writer/producer.

He received an award for Social Network.

Sony was also talking to David Fincher, the director.

We were actually talking to a team Marcos had put together at that time.

It was when we got the word back about Wozniak.

Rodriguez

Yeah, one of our guys, David, had somebody on the same block as Wozniak and we were in cell phone contact with David as he watched the street.

Actually, what happens is Wozniak is a decent fellow, but his wife has become a gatekeeper for him.

So, when she left the house we would ring his phone; but we were too late as he was already in Sony's camp.

It's a classic Hollywood story.

Hulme

We made him an offer but we were too late.

We didn't really need him as we had the script and we just needed him for public relations and to consult.

When we cast Wozniak with Josh Gad, Wozniak went online saying that we made a good casting call.

He has not been a part of Apple for a long time and he left Apple before Jobs was fired.

I hear he actually waits in line to get the latest Apple products.

Is not that weird?

Here he is an Apple founder but he waits in line to get the latest iPHONE.

That is really weird!

His title is cofounder, but that was long ago.

Bower

Mark, listening to your story and how this is not normally what you do, but you said you had a lot of experience in what not to do.

You said you had all the right pieces in the right places and all the right people in the right seats on the bus... how did you learn that,

and what period of time did it take to learn it?

Hulme

Well, I am sure we spent more than we should have and yet, today, I am not sure we learned anything.

In this particular case all the stars just lined up.

Marcos can back me up, it hasn't been a smooth ride.

We hit all the potholes.

But we never slammed into an immovable wall.

We just kept on going.

At one time I had to back down: the only thing we had to agree to when we signed Ashton was we would spend at least $500,000 on advertising.

And that wasn't close, we actually had to spend well over $6,000,000... and I bowed down to the experienced folks in the industry... so I don't know whether we really learned anything.

[Laughter]

I am being honest with you.

I keep wishing and hoping I have and that's why I want to do a second movie.

[Laughter]

Jones

Mark, you spoke about two million and that went out the window... I don't mean you blew it, but what is the current burn rate?

How much money have you spent?

And whose money is it?

Hulme

It is a combination.

Once it got to a certain point, I said this is all I am willing to risk.

I really don't want to risk taking everything down chasing a movie.

Wouldn't that be embarrassing?

I am in the foreclosure business and now the lead story in magazines and in our mass meeting would be about me... wouldn't that be embarrassing?

So I have some friends who have done some land deals together and I approached them about coming on board.

We had always been concerned about each others investments so we were family in a way.

So, we went to my entertainment attorney and he showed me how it's done in the entertainment industry to bring in investors.

When I saw it, I said Frank that is dumb, I will not do it that way.

It is dumb, so we didn't do it.

The only real partners are the director, Joshua Michael Stern, and Ashton - both of them get a piece of the backend.

Everything else is just part of the LLC.

The burn rate is... John Spargo, it is so frustrating, you could produce a film for under $500,000, and I know you can do that.

But right now I am facing a bill for $200,000 to do color correcting for the lighting.

Imagine that!!!

I have a great director of photography but no I need another $200,000 just to get the color corrected.

Rodriguez

You ask, "Why didn't you get the color right when you were shooting it?"

Hulme

Absolutely, let me tell you: the big pictures you see are all made or lost in the post production.

I am not talking about special effects.

No I am talking about a simple movie with no special effects.

On the set they only capture the data and the film comes alive in the back room during post production.

My guess now is my $2 million will be somewhere around $12 million... this is what happens in this crazy business.

I asked my foreign sales agency, "Looks like we are destined to make money... right?", and they said yes... so I said, "If I was to quit now, would I be the only person in the industry who made one film and made money and quit?"

I was thinking about Las Vegas, where you go in and pull one lever, hit the jackpot and go home and never ever return.

So would I be the only Hollywood producer that made money on 100% of the films?

They said Absolutely, hands down!

[Laughter]

The only guy that batted 1,000... that's better than Ted Williams. But I would have to have the discipline to quit.

Reuven

If you did they would end up making a movie about Mark Hulme. It would be like the first Rocky movie.

[Laughter]

Mancuso

Mark, how much would you take to bow out now and sell the movie?

After all this is a business and unless you suddenly become emotionally involved there should be a magic number you would take to sell what you created.

If MGM came to you today and say we will give $30,000,000 to walk away now - yes or No to thirty million?

A cash deal.

Hulme

Well, if they agree to buy a final film and they will not reshoot it; and you said cash, right?

Mancuso

Yes.

Hulme

If they don't rip it apart and go reshoot it, yeah, I would hand it off for thirty million.

Well not thirty million, I will not to get my original money back as well, so let's say $32, 500,000.

I do not really know what I would take to turn it over but no one has offered big money... yet.

[Laughter]

Jones

Hello, Mark and Marcos, it's been an honor to be here this weekend and listen to this story.

I want to thank you both.

You know, I take a ribbing from my fellow British CEOs about having to fly across the pond to get CEO advice.

They always say why not be like the rest of us and come down the pub one night and you will get more advice in an hour; while you fly two wasted days just back and forth as part of the Super PAC.

Plus I have never missed a Super PAC meeting in ten years.

Mark, if Steve Jobs is looking down now, he would be proud of what you are doing.

He would be proud of how you are going about this as you really do think differently.

Now, outside of the country that this man lived and was born in, it's already in the black; so you have amazingly accomplish good things by thinking out of the box.

You are another one of those folks who are going to change the world.

You already have a real vote of confidence and don't lose sleep over the domestic market.

The International market maybe twice as big as normal for this movie.

Steve Jobs is huge worldwide.

Bear in mind that in numbers we have spoken about, we went from $2 million to $5 million, to $6 million, and finally to $12 million.

We did that in the space of an hour, I know it took you longer.

In the movie business, things are weird.

This is normal.

I learned that from you today.

So, lets get a cutting edge, San Francisco type marketing firm to get this message out virally for you.

Do it in a new way, don't follow what is normal.

You have followed that path already.

Its like the shinny new car that's not been unveiled and it has the sheet over and suddenly a beauty in a bight red bikini pulls the sheet off the car and varooom... there it is!

It might only cost you $50,000 to do that and that is a small number when you make it part of the $13 million budget.

It's a small beer as compared to what you have blown so far.

But I don't mean you have "blown it"... it's an investment.

I like the idea of getting the geeks and the Steve Jobs fan club folks aboard as early adopters of the movie.

See if you could give these folks snippets of the film which were cut and never used.

You know, we get Ashton Kutcher sitting in the old garage and the lights are low and it looks like he is working on something new... what is it?

This is my last input on my one answer response, I have just broken my single piece of advice into smaller pieces.

I think you have stumbled on something about making a movie into a business.

So when you said a scene has to have a specific budget, that's new thinking and its not movie people thinking.

If you go over your budget for a scene you get fired... that is completely new thinking for the movie industry.

I think that's really new thinking and why shouldn't you become the guru who brings this type of thinking to the movie industry?

Go advise producer planning on making a movie for $150,000,000 and say, "I will show you how to do it for half".

Then you share in the savings.

I know that's something down the road or around the corner but if your Jobs movie fails, this cost cutting/budgeting will be a new business for you.

I wish you a lot of luck and I am going to make a prediction right now that you are going to make $500,000,000 and that you will be a smashing success.

_____

Hulme

Thanks for the prediction, I am going to hold you to it and next time we are together I will expect you to make up any shortfall... ok?

_____

Glosser

First I want to say thank you for having Mike and I present as your story is touching.

I think you joined the CEO Club about the time we bought a little ten person machine shop in Dallas.

We are practically neighbors.

We want to extend you an anytime invitation to see our shop.

Today we have a four-hundred thousand square foot facility and we are a full service contact manufacturer.

Some day you may need to have one of your ideas turned into a finished product and we would be pleased to help you.

I want to congratulate you as a true person who thinks different and wants to change the world.

Congratulations.

Mike Powell (Gayle Glosser's husband)

Yes, I feel the same way, it's been a pleasure listening to how you went through the process step by step, and I echo Gayle's comments.

It has been enlightening as it is informative.

I will look forward to seeing the movie.

Like Roy, I think Steve Jobs would be proud of what you have done with his life.

I especially enjoyed you having a "Steve Jobs moment", and I think someone should do a book on you or at least an article.

I am proud to know you.

Mark, everything I am about to say disregard.

[Laughter]

But listen anyway because there could be something I say that's valuable.

Anyway, I heard from other Super PAC sessions that advice is for giving and not for taking.

Sell that sucker.

Get rid of it.

[Laughter]

Get rid of it right now.

But, before I would sell it I would be talking to the folks that get you on Jay Leno or David Letterman.

If it's not you, use a spokesman.

Joe could do it for you.

And I would hype it... hype it... hype it... it would be much better than sliced bread.

I would sell it, I would make a little money; and I do not want you to be a one hit wonder.

I want you to see if you like that crap, working side by side with those buttholes - do you like that stuff? - and when you got your money out do it again.

You will find another deal, but get your money out.

You can never lose money by taking a profit.

[Laughter]

Hulme

Wait a minute, I want to write that down.

[Laughter]

Pruitt

How did that conservative TV Bill Riley or Bill O'Reilly do it?

First, he wrote a book on Lincoln, now he wrote one on JFK.

How do they promote their stuff? - it's not as good as yours, so I want you to hype it, really hype it!

Hype that thing right now and then sell it.

Take that cash off the table, put it in your pocket.

Then if you like that crap, do it again.

Milli Brown of Brown Books in Dallas is also in the CEO Clubs.

I don't know if she knows up from down about movies, but she sure knows books.

You are practically neighbors.

Go see her and tell her we should do a book on Steve Jobs and then tell her we should do a book on Mark Hulme.

That is her business.

Just go see her.

I probably have said more than I should, but just hype it and take your money off the table.

Layne

Joe, this analog voice recorder is more than thirty years old.

If Steve Jobs sees me holding an analog tape recorder in my hand, he will roll over in his grave.

Joe, where the hell did you get this antique?

You could sell it on Pawn Stars as an antique.

[Everyone takes turns talking into a handheld tape recorder]

Mark, I doubt whether you will ever be able to hear this audio tape because you can't find anything to play it on.

First of all, thanks for sharing this as it is incredibly enlightening.

I think we are all jealous of the fun you had doing this and I can see now how the CEO Club says... we are in the business of making money and having fun all while we are learning.

It really sounds like you have had a lot of fun.

Here are a few quick ideas...

First the syndicated morning radio show, Imus in the morning has a huge following and all you have to do is call in to get the message out.

The author of the Jobs book, Isaacson, was on Imus in the morning and the audience is hundreds of thousands.

The second thing I would do is collect Jobs testimonials.

I would start now to collect them from Joan Baez, Bob Dylan, Bill Gates, everybody.

I think Jobs creates an incredible sucking sound and I would start interviewing all the people he worked with as it will only grow more valuable over time.

You could do these interviews online and you could play it five times a week on HBO.

That's a terrific way to get exposure to the movie.

Mancuso

What a fun day we have all had and tonight we will have dinner together under the beautiful sunset in Santa Fe.

I just want to mention how lucky we all are.

Really, when we sit here and spend the weekend together it's easy to forget there is a lot of trouble in the world and a whole lot of folks who are hurting.

It is so easy to forget how lucky each of us is and not be grateful for our luck.

Oh, sure we have some unique skills but we all know that luck is the hardest skill to learn and acquire.

In my 37th year as founder of the CEO Clubs, today has to rank among our most entertaining and educationally fulfilling days.

I sure have had fun today.

Now, I turn over this cheap analog tape recorder as an antique to Mark for the final word.

He has suffered through another Super PAC and the good news is he is still alive... Mark?

Hulme

A great day.

I received advice to sell and advice to keep going.

Perfect.

Now I am really happy because I cannot make a bad choice.

So, let me tell you what I am doing.

Dave, let me say I appreciate your advice and that's one of those things that in hindsight you say, wish I had taken that advice.

I am here for a reason and I am here in spirit of Steve Jobs.

Jobs would never have taken the money.

So I am afraid I have to honor him on that topic.

Mancuso

What about if it's cash.

Hulme

Then if it's cash, I will have dishonor him.

[Laughter]

Unfortunately, a little bit of money doesn't help you with your next project.

It's such a cash-sucking business.

I will keep you posted on that.

You know, I am absolutely touched that I have been such a backslider in the CEO Clubs and you all allowed me to come back and dominate the meeting.

Really, I am touched by that show of support.

It is really inspiring.

To think you folks would spend this much time with me is deeply appreciated.

I must also say, it has been therapeutic and cathartic.

I have never done anything like this before.

Especially with Marcos.

It is the first time we ever just sat down and went through the story from front to back.

Plus, to do this with all successful CEOs and entrepreneurs makes it even more dramatic.

Of course, that is one of the verticals we are targeting with our movie.

Sure we are targeting the Mac heads but I respect the business mentality of this type group of successful CEOs and entrepreneurs.

This business mentality is just missing from the industry and it benefits from a non-industry person to come in and do something totally different.

This has really been great, as this is the very first time I have been able to just talk to business people.

Really, it has been great.

I have tremendous respect for what all of you have accomplished and I am humbled that you would sit with me for this long a period and let me dominate.

I have been such a backslider.

So, to all of you, Thanks.

I am going to extend this invitation, for whatever it is worth: be my guests at our premiers.

You know those premiers are big events, hot tickets.

We will surely have the full cast in Los Angeles and Palo Alto (that's where he was born) and New York.

I will work with Joe to coordinate but I would be honored if you all can make the premiers.

It will be so fun to have this group reassemble for the premiers.

Remember we are still not done with the film.

We are still in that vulnerable phase where we don't have the distribution story but to get to that place will be a blast.

To do this would be a blast.

Let me give you a few of our marketing ideas which we can discuss over dinner or the next few days.

Actually, this is one of Ashton's ideas: instead of releasing the previews and material to the media, make it only an exclusive release to the iPHONE app downloader.

It will be free, but this way you will actually get it first.

To honor Steve Jobs we will give these folks little teasers and trailers before we give it to the media.

You know we are all electronically connected and soon a lot of those brands will start to fade because you just do not need them.

Soon you will be able to pick and choose what channel you want.

I have tons of ideas and there isn't enough time to comment on them.

So, from the bottom of my heart, thank you all so very much for this experience.

———————————

[Applause]

The following review of the movie jOBS was received on 1/26/13 from Super PAC member, Cash Nickerson…

Ashton Kutcher Kicks Ass As

Steve Jobs In Indie Film, jOBS!

A Critical Review by Cash Nickerson

I have only been to Park City, Utah twice in my 50 plus years, both occasioned by my 20 year friendship with Marcos Rodriguez, a role model of an entrepreneur. On this second occasion, I was a guest of Mark Hulme's company, Five Star Productions, to attend the debut of jOBS at the Sundance Film Festival. My relationship with the two Marks originated with Joe Mancuso's CEO Club, a unique collection of entrepreneurs. Hulme is the Producer and Marcos one of the executive producers. Sitting in the Eccles Theatre with Marcos as we watched his name on the silver screen was a moving experience of itself.

Congratulations to the two Mark's and all those associated with the film, especially Ashton Kutcher and director Joshua Michael Stern for putting together a fascinating collection of thought provoking scenes with an "it is what it is" biopic on Steve Jobs.

The film is not what one is used to in the way of Hollywood fare. It doesn't feel compelled to give some tidy, wrap it in a package and put a ribbon around it before it is over explanation of who jOBS was and why. In this way, I suspect some traditional Hollywood critics may think it could use some editing to make it tighter and more slick. But this very feeling of watching this bundle of sometimes disconnected scenes gets you into Steve Jobs head which after the movie looks to have been a complicated space full of dichotomy, negative impossibility, solipsism, anger and relentlessness as if he knew he would someday die too young.

Ashton Kutcher did a magnificent job of portraying Steve Jobs. And yes it helps that there is some resemblance, which is mesmerizing at times. But you can see Ashton worked at this. In the Q and A following the screening he admitted to adopting Jobs fruitarian diet and ended up in the hospital with an issue with his pancreas. That is method acting that almost went too far. What impressed me about Ashton's performance was his range. The spectrum of emotions required the ability to reflect hope, hatred, anger, detachment, cruelty, altered state of consciousness, depression, selfishness, triumph and revenge. Whether he is screaming at Bill Gates for his "criminal" copying of the MacIntosh or listening to Stevw Wozniak resign with total detachment, Kutcher is beyond believable in his portrayal. Gads by the way is absolutely phenomenol in his channelling of Wozniak.

But in the end, with so much screen time, this is Ashton's to win or lose-and I believe he wins. I spoke with Ashton at the premier party and complimented him on his range. We share a jiu jitsu instructor in LA, my dear friendRigan Machado and he trains from time to time at The Academy in Beverly Hills in which I am a partner. Rigan is an 8 time

world champ in Brazilian Jiu Jitsu and throws me around like a killer whale. Ashton and I joked about Rigan and his closing words as I shook his hand goodnight were, " I am going to kick Rigan's ass,". If Ashton puts the focus and energy he put into jOBS, he will be a champ at BJJ someday as we'll.

An Entrepreneurial Tale

A fairy tale usually starts out "once upon a time", and entrepreneurial tale often begins with "you are not going to believe this shit".

I am about to share an entrepreneurial tale about one of the Super PAC members who are featured in this book. Please observe many of the members chose not to attend the filming session in Santa Fe where this material was developed.

There are, as usual, multiple reasons for their absence. Most are a function of not wanting to be visible to a camera. Some have security clearances which would be at risk for little gain. Others simply had travel and schedule issues, as Santa Fe is not an airline hub. Although I should add, it is such a lovely town everyone should spend some time in the art galleries.

The story begins as a Super PAC member begins his career as an airline stewardess flying between NY and Hong Kong. He used to say, coffee, tea or me. He is and was a terrific talent and quick witted.

On one trip to Hong Kong, he had an extended layover and decided to visit mainland China and the port city of Shenzhen.

As he drove about in awe he saw signs saying "Mission Hills 180 holes". He soon learned about China famous ten golf courses at one location. He decided to stay over one night at the resort and enjoy his extended stay. He met the Vancouver based owner of the resort at a breakfast, Tenniel Chu and his second son. The conversation soon drifted to Chinese businesses seeking to expand.

Our flight attendant had no prior significant business experience but passionately wanted to be an entrepreneur. He just was not in a position to launch a business and had just completed his tenth year with the airline. Mr. Chu suggested that one the best golfers at Mission Hill was also the owner of a bicycle factory in Shenzhen, Philipp Tong. He suggested the flight attendant visit the bicycle plant.

The next day he walked in the lobby and said, "I would like to buy some bicycles". Those are magic words. Three hours later he signed a purchase order for $500,000 worth of assorted bicycles. While he had no business experience, he was innately a hell-u-va negotiator. Besides placing the order, he negotiated the terms as payable in ninety days. Now that is a good negotiator and an entrepreneur in the making. He likes to say, an entrepreneur plays by the rules when he wins, and when he loses he just changes the rules so he can win.

Armed with the purchase order, as soon as he returned home his first visit was to Toys 'r us. He told them about a unique opportunity to expand their bicycle line at very, very favorable prices. He also told them at these drastically reduced prices, he would need payment in thirty days.

And so a business was born.

After all, what is the only ingredient that is both necessary and sufficient to start a business? No, it is not money, passion, or experience. It is a customer.

Five years later, after several years of multi-million dollars of earning, he joined the www.ceoclubs.org Super PAC group.

Overcoming Problems

A few months after the launch of this new business our flight attendant, who was upgraded to a first class attendant, had still not left the security of his job and guaranteed paycheck. Entrepreneurs must overcome all problems as they occur and the hero of this story faced a real crisis.

On his flight back to the USA, he watched Philipp Tong, the owner of the bicycle business where he had a 90 day advance of $500,000 settle into a first class seat. His heart pounded. While his flight attendant outfit was recently pressed, his face was white as the blood drained from his body. He panicked.

He did what anybody else would do.....he left the plane and vomited in the boarding area. He quit his job right then and there.

He felt so much better when the flight was in the air. But, he then discovered he was alone in Hong Kong, without any money and no return flight to the USA.

We leave the story here and ask the reader to decide which of these statements are true...

1) This is a made up story.
2) This is the disguised back ground of one of the folks in the book.
3) Everything is true as is.
4) Half is true, half is made-up.

Largest Box Office Bombs (Losses Adjusted For Inflation)

Rank	Title	Year	Net Losses
1	Shanghai Surprise	1986	$31,133,962
2	Exit to Eden	1994	$31,608,998
3	Larger than Life	1996	$32,171,194
4	Glitter	2001	$32,456,810
5	There Be Dragons	2011	$32,675,365
6	Dangerous Ground	1997	$32,709,642
7	The Warrior's Way	2010	$32,945,585
8	The Black Cauldron	1985	$33,059,341
9	The Stupids	1996	$33,466,900
10	Pushing Tin	1999	$34,307,770

Pac And Super PAC

(Presidential Advisory Councils)

A PAC (Presidential Advisory Council) is a group of about a dozen CEO members who serve as a board of advisors for one another - A "mastermind" group or a wolf-pack.

About 150 CEO Club members participate in a PAC. PAC members must be members of the CEO Club. PAC members must sign mutual confidentiality agreements, agree to share detailed financial information, and agree not to miss more than two consecutive meetings. They also must be in control of their company and need to have a minimum of 25 employees with at least $2 million in annual sales.

Sounding out issues or decisions with a knowledgeable, yet not directly involved, peer group can significantly improve the odds of success.

The group focuses on the host company's biggest problem or opportunities. The council then offers solutions and advice. A mastermind

occurs at the end of each session as each member shares their ideas to aid the host. This is audio-taped for the host to utilize as a reference. Confidentiality agreements are signed due to the sharing of financial information. Meetings include recaps and current developments by the council members present.

A PAC meets eight times annually, at each member's business. Each meeting usually goes from 10am to 5pm.

The Super PAC is for larger companies and operates on an international basis. Minimum company size is $10 million in annual sales. Super PACs meet for three-day weekends three times a year. Annual fees are in excess of $10,000 for two people. All Super PAC members receive all the benefits of a full CEO Club member.

The CEO Clubs Top Ten Audio Luncheon Talks

Plus, Mancuso's 10 Tips For Writing A Wining Business Plan

*Frank "Catch Me If You Can" Abagnale
*Bill Bartmann — Bankrupt Billionaires
*Jack Canfield — Chicken Soup Of The Soul
*Kurt Eichenwald — Enron
*Bernard Harris — Astronaut
*Joe Mancuso — Business Plans
*Pat McGovern — IDG
*David Neeleman — JetBlue
*Tony Parinello — Selling to VITO
*Pete Peterson — Blackstone
*Ted Turner — Outrageous!

Why are these eleven more popular than our other favorites: Herb Kelleher, Southwest airlines; Zig Ziglar, inspirational speaker; Mike Bloomberg, Mayor Of New York; Steve Forbes; Ken Fisher; Fred Smith? Members seem to find these messages an enjoyable way to learn and now these are all transferable to a Smartphone in one minute.

"Over the past thirty-five years, The CEO CLUBS have sponsored hundreds of luncheons appealing to CEOs of companies with average annual sales of about $20,000,000. If you attended all the luncheons, you would have spent about $60,000. Of course you would have enjoyed drinks and lunch and the company of your peers. We have converted over 200 of these luncheons talks to MP3 format and placed them on the website. You can download them for an MP3 player or order the CD. Here are the eleven most popular talks. Some of these are truly jewels and like a good wine, they age well. They are a mini MBA program."

Go to http://www.ceoclubs.org to find out more.

THE ENTREPRENEURIAL QUIZ

While there is no single entrepreneurial archetype, there are certain character traits that indicate an entrepreneurial personality. In this quiz, developed from a series of questionnaire analyses performed by the Center for Entrepreneurial Management, we've concentrated on those indicators. If you've ever wondered whether or not you have what it takes to be an entrepreneur, here's your chance to find out.

This extremely popular self-diagnostic test was first produced in 1984 in a best selling book:

How To Start, Finance, And Manage Your Own Small Business
Author: Joseph R. Mancuso
ISBN: 9780671763565
Publisher: Simon & Schuster

It has been reproduced hundreds of times as parts of other books and millions and millions of times in article in newspapers and magazines.

Because Apple was founded in 1976, we thought this quiz, which was developed around the same time, was an appropriate inclusion to this book.

*You can get the answers to this quiz at:

http://www.ceoclubs.org/section/resources.php

Begin

1. How were your parents employed?

   a. Both worked and were self-employed for most of their working lives

   b. Both worked and were self-employed for some part of their working lives

   c. One parent was self employed for most of his or her working life

   d. One parent was self-employed at some point in his or her working life

   e. Neither parent was ever self-employed

2. Have you ever been fired from a job?

   a. Yes, more than once

   b. Yes, once

   c. No

3. Are you an immigrant, or were your parents or grandparents immigrants?

   a. I was born outside the United States

   b. One or both of my parents were born outside of the United States

    c.   At least one of my grandparents was born outside of the United States

    d.   Does not apply

4. Your work career has been:

    a.   Primarily in small business (under 100 employees)

    b.   Primarily in medium-size business (101 to 500 employees)

    c.   Primarily in big business (over 500 employees)

5. How many businesses did you operate before you were twenty?

    a.   Many

    b.   A few

    c.   None

6. What is your present age?

    a.   21-30

    b.   31-40

    c.   41-50

    d.   51 or over

7. You are the _____ child in the family

    a.   oldest

    b.   middle

    c.   youngest

    d.   other

8. What is your marital status?

    a.   Married

    b.   Divorced

    c.   Single

9. Your highest level of formal education is:
   a. Some high school
   b. High school diploma
   c. Bachelor's degree
   d. Master's degree
   e. Doctorate

10. What is your primary motivation in starting a business?
    a. To make money
    b. I don't like working for someone else
    c. To be famous
    d. To have an outlet for excess energy

11. Your relationship with the parent who provided most of the family's income was:
    a. Strained
    b. Comfortable
    c. Competitive
    d. Nonexistent

12. If you could choose between working hard and working smart, you would:
    a. Work hard
    b. Work smart
    c. Both

13. On whom do you rely for critical management advice?
    a. Internal management teams
    b. External management professionals
    c. External financial professionals
    d. No one except myself

14. If you were at the racetrack, which of these would you bet on?
    a. The daily double - a chance to make a killing
    b. A ten-to-one shot
    c. A three-to-one shot
    d. The two-to-one favorite

15. The only ingredient that is both necessary and sufficient for starting a business is:
    a. Money
    b. Customers
    c. An idea or product
    d. Motivation and hard work

16. If you were an advanced tennis player and had a chance to play a top pro like Jimmy Connors, you would:
    a. Turn it down because he could beat you
    b. Accept the challenge, but not bet any money on it
    c. Bet a week's pay that you would win
    d. Get odds, bet a fortune, and try for an upset

17. You tend to "fall in love" to quickly with:
    a. New product ideas.
    b. New employees.
    c. New manufacturing ideas.
    d. New financial plans.
    e. All of the above.

18. Which of the following personality types is best suited to be your right-hand person?
    a. Bright and energetic.

    b.   Bright and lazy.

    c.   Dumb and energetic.

19. You accomplish tasks better because:
    a.   You are always on time.
    b.   You are super organized.
    c.   You keep good records.

20. You hate to discuss:
    a.   Problems involving employees.
    b.   Signing expense accounts.
    c.   New management practices.
    d.   The future of the business.

21. Given a choice, you would prefer:
    a.   Rolling dice with a one-in-three chance of winning.
    b.   Working on a problem with a one-in-three chance of solving it in the allotted time.

22. If you could choose between the following competitive professions, your choice would be:
    a.   Professional golf.
    b.   Sales.
    c.   Personnel counseling.
    d.   Teaching.

23. If you had to choose between working with a partner who is a close friend and working with a stranger who is an expert in your field, your choice would be:
    a.   The close friend.
    b.   The expert.

24. In business situations that demand action, clarifying who is in charge will help produce results:
    a. Agree.
    b. Agree, with reservations.
    c. Disagree.

25. In playing a competitive game, you are concerned with:
    a. How well you play.
    b. Winning or losing.
    c. Both of the above.
    d. Neither of the above.

*You can get the answers to this quiz at:
    http://www.ceoclubs.org/section/resources.php

MOTIVATIONAL PROFILE OF AN ENTREPRENEUR
Achievement, Affiliation, and Power
The Entrepreneurial Profile Assessment Exercise

Before delving into the motivational profile of the entrepreneur, we believe each one of you should answer the following questions as objectively as possible, in order to best understand your own motivations in the world of entrepreneurship.

Begin
Please answer each question as it pertains to you. As you read the questions, please put a number besides the question. Your choice of numbers are 7, 5, 4, 3, 1 with 7 meaning fully agree, 1 meaning fully disagree and 4 meaning in the middle.

1. I love to be together with people I like even when it serves no purpose. ____
2. In many situations, clarifying who is in charge is the most important business at hand. ____
3. When playing a game, I am as concerned with how well I play in my own estimation as I am with whether or not I win. ____
4. I believe it is most important to have the respect of others in your community. ____
5. When I set a goal, there is a good chance I will make it even though it doesn't always happen. ____
6. It is important to have possessions that will influence others to respect me. ____
7. Losing a friend is very upsetting to me. I work hard to regain friends I have lost. ____
8. I insist on the respect of people under me, even if I have to push them around to get it. ____
9. I need lots of warmth from others and I give it back. ____
10. I think about how what I am doing today will affect my future five years from now. ____
11. I like to set up measures for myself of how well I am progressing. ____
12. I am very concerned with the efficiency and quality of my work. ____
13. Many people need advice and help, and someone should give it to them whether they want it or not. ____
14. Strong actions are needed when people make mistakes. ____
15. I enjoy social get-togethers and make time to go to them. ____
16. A key purpose in my life is to do things that have not been done before. ____
17. If I move to a new area, I imagine the first thing I would do is develop new friends, I'm like a plant without water. ____

18. I intend to get strong emotional reactions out of others because I know I am getting somewhere. ___

19. I need very much to be liked by others. ___

20. My friends may sometimes think it dull, but I find myself talking about how to overcome future obstacles I have anticipated. ___

21. My close relationships are very valuable to me. ___

22. My reason for being in business is to become rich, rich, rich! ___

23. I don't like working on a project without knowing how well I'm doing, so I make plans that allow me to measure how fast I'm proceeding toward my overall goals. ___

24. I like to get involved in community activities because it gives me a chance to have influence where I live. ___

25. The real meaning of life is the personal relationships we form. ___

26. I do best when I have some room to choose my own goals. ___

27. If people don't know you really appreciate them, you can't expect them to do a good job. ___

28. In everything I do; work, sports, hobbies, I try to set really high standards for myself; otherwise where's the fun of it? ___

29. Its people that make up a business, not a lot of stock piled up on the shelves. ___

30. I always thought I would enjoy being a famous politician, actor or athlete and live in the lap of luxury. ___

Motivational Profile Evaluation

These questions, all 30 of them, can be subdivided into three equal groups: Achievement, Affiliation, and Power. While all tests are fairly limited in scope, this test, or evaluation, can be decoded by treating the questions listed as per the key below. Mark down your rating (1, 3, 4, 5, or 7) by each question. Then, please add the scores in each column to get the total score for each category of need.

ACHIEVEMENT

Question #3 _____

Question #5 _____

Question #10 _____

Question #11 _____

Question #12 _____

Question #16 _____

Question #20 _____

Question #23 _____

Question #26 _____

Question #28 _____

TOTAL ACHIEVEMENT SCORE: _____

AFFILIATION

Question #1 _____

Question #6 _____

Question #9 _____

Question #15 _____

Question #17 _____

Question #19 _____

Question #21 _____

Question #25 _____

Question #27 _____

Question #29 _____

    TOTAL AFFILIATION SCORE: _____

POWER

Question #2 _____

Question #4 _____

Question #6 _____

Question #8 _____

Question #13 _____

Question #14 _____

Question #18 _____

Question #22 _____

Question #24 _____

Question #30 _____

    TOTAL POWER SCORE: _____

Highest-Grossing Films (Adjusted For Inflation)

Rank	Title	Year	Worldwide gross
1	Gone with the Wind	1939	$3,301,400,000
2	Avatar	2009	$2,782,300,000
3	Star Wars	1977	$2,710,800,000
4	Titanic	1997	$2,413,800,000
5	The Sound of Music	1965	$2,269,800,000
6	E.T. the Extra-Terrestrial	1982	$2,216,800,000
7	The Ten Commandments	1956	$2,098,600,000
8	Doctor Zhivago	1965	$1,988,600,000
9	Jaws	1975	$1,945,100,000
10	Snow White and the Seven Dwarfs	1937	$1,746,100,000

Do you want to see this book as a movie?

Certainly you should see the Ashton Kutcher film.

The dialogue in this book is drawn 99% from an entrepreneurial documentary film with the same title as this book. In October 2012, a group of CEO enjoyed a detailed roundtable discussion with the entrepreneur who decided to venture into moviemaking. It was his first effort and the dialogue is delicious.

Text and photos are no substitute for body language and the 70 minute case study is informative and entertaining.

To see this documentary by D.V.D. or download or streaming go to
www.ceoclubs.org
http://www.ceoclubs.org/

Printed in the USA
CPSIA information can be obtained
at www.ICGtesting.com
JSHW012012140824
68134JS00024B/2381

9 781614 488866